RAINWATER HARVESTING AND USE

UNDERSTANDING THE BASICS OF RAINWATER HARVESTING

A. ZAGELOW

Rainwater Harvesting and Use

A Guide

Understanding the Basics of Rainwater Harvesting

Table of Contents

<u>Click Here to Download Your *FREE* Copies of our Greywater Harvesting Guide & Sustainable Living Strategies Checklist</u>

How to Use This Book

Great effort has been taken to give the reader practical, concise and actionable information from which to design a high-quality rainwater harvesting system that will be in service for years to come. In some cases, related sections may contain overlapping information which is done on purpose to emphasis importance and relevance to the entire system. Each chapter builds on the previous one but for easy reference each chapter has a summary highlighting the important points covered. This book is for the Do-It-Yourself homeowner or for the person who just wants to be able to have an informed conversation with an installing contractor.

Wading in...

Although water abundantly covers 71% of our planet less than 1% is suitable for human consumption. The shortage of clean water is still one of the most-overwhelming problems that the world continues to face in the 21st century. The issues contributing to this situation are complex but include a variety of geographic and political challenges that inhibit the efficient and equitable distribution of safe potable water. Difficulties in accessing safe water is a growing issue for millions of people all over the world that is resulting in serious health problems and even death.

Along with difficultly of access, there are other reasons that lead to lack of clean water. Environmental pollution, disappearance of water sources (lakes and rivers running dry), draughts, flooding's that pollute water, over pumping of aquifers, lack of access or good water distribution systems along with the inadequate filtration and management of water. In a drought situation, an area not only faces scarcity of water, but brackish groundwater and polluted surface water, making the available water unsafe for domestic use.

Currently, annual deficits of clean water continue to rise, even in the United States, which in 1972 approved the Clean Water Act with one of its main focuses being to improve water quality. Several major rivers are running dry all over the entire planet, such as the Colorado River, Indus, Yellow, and Rio Grande that at certain times of the year may have entire dry sections in their body. Moreover, the activity of water mining, can decrease aquifer water tables up to 10 feet per year. In addition, the Natural Resources Defense Council reported that pollution is already affecting the drinking water systems in the US cities.

Clean water is essential for domestic routines as well as for the future development in various sectors of agriculture and industry. Water is imbued in every aspect of the complex chain of processes that brings everyone all the goods and services we enjoy. We will see the results of the growing water crisis in ways we don't yet comprehend as supply chains find it harder to get to the consumers their desired consumables. So, how well do you know your current local clean water situation?

A statement published in 2000 from the World Resources Institutes states that "by the end of 2025, approximately 3.5 billion people - about half the world's population; will live in areas without enough water for agriculture, industry, and human needs globally. Furthermore, there is going to be a decrease in water quality in all regions including the ones with intensive agriculture, and large urban and/or industrial areas."

Why Do We Need Rainwater Harvesting?

The water needs of the planet are increasing at an exponential rate, therefore, pressure is increasing to develop alternative water supplies to meet the shortage of potable water affecting the entire planet. The necessity of a steady flow of accessible water that can be easily disseminated to fulfill various needs is required not only for human consumption but for all ecosystems.

The most recurring and permanent source of safe water is rainwater. Thus, harvesting it allows us to preserve it for present and future use with relative simplicity in its collection, storage and implementation. Rainwater harvesting can be described as an activity that involves the collection of rainwater from a catchment area and then transferring it for storage in ponds, tanks or barrels. It then can be used for meeting residential needs with something as simple as a couple of rain barrels to more sophisticated commercial and industrial needs where large cisterns and pumping skids are used. Therefore, rainwater harvesting can be successfully used as an alternative and/or supplement to municipal water sources allowing it as a complement to conventional technologies to achieve consistency in water supplies.

WATER

1 in 9 people lack access to safe water

Before going any further, it is important to mention that rainwater harvesting is not a new concept, it has been used for centuries all over the world such as in places like China, Israel, Sri Lanka and Uganda, and currently, new generations of converts are embracing rainwater harvesting as well.

It is believed banana leaves were the first rainwater harvesting systems to be used. This ancient technique can collect as much as 50+ gallons (200 liters) of water in a single rainfall and is still used in several developing countries even today. Rainwater harvesting provides a flexible and easily accessible source of water that has been collected and stored.

Rainwater harvesting techniques have been re-introduced in local and regional areas, but its usage remains largely underused due to lack of education and innovation. Many end users are unaware about the technical and financial requirements of the process. This book will help aid in your understanding of the basics of rainwater harvesting and is a comprehensive reference for the beginner to intelligently implement it at the residential level.

Understanding the Advantages and Disadvantages of Rainwater Harvesting

Advantages of Rainwater

The list of advantages is long, most of which we will discuss more in depth in chapters to follow.

- It's free
- Superior purity & softness
- Nearly neutral pH
- Salt free
- Mineral free
- Free from disinfection by-products
- Free of other and natural contaminates
- Plants flourish when irrigated with it
- Extends life of appliances – low corrosiveness and scaling
- Simple & low-cost catchment/conveyance/distribution/storage systems
- Alternate source in emergencies – Water security
- Predictable annual augmentation to existing sources
- Eliminates need and cost for water softener
- Reduces storm water runoff and erosion caused by it
- Lowers utility bills
- Lowers demand on storm sewers and treatment plants

Disadvantages of Rainwater

The biggest disadvantage of harvesting rainwater is that it can being wildly inconsistent, hence difficult to accurately predict and manage. In Chapter 3: How to Design a Rainwater Harvesting System, I provide you with tools and techniques to help you accurately calculate your harvest potential and mitigate the impact of dry spells.

The second disadvantage of rainwater harvesting is being responsible for the operation and maintenance of the system. Those responsibilities include:

- Overall operation and maintenance checks of the system at regular intervals. During heavier rains daily/weekly checks are recommended weekly/monthly checks during lighter and less frequent rainfall.
  - Regular purging of the first flush system
  - Cleaning of the catchment surface
  - Cleaning of the reservoirs
- Potable systems include additional maintenance such as:
  - Pump maintenance
  - Replacement of filter media
  - Maintenance of disinfection equipment
  - Regular testing of the water

I personally don't consider maintaining a rainwater harvesting system a disadvantage especially with all the advantages you gain. All systems in the built environment require some level of maintenance and with a well thought out maintenance schedule it can be easy and rewarding.

Chapter Summary

1. Less than 1% of the Earth's water is suitable for human consumption (Potable).

2. Rainwater harvesting systems have been around for almost a millennium, possibly longer.

3. Political and geographic challenges are the main contributors that inhibit efficient, safe and equitable distribution of potable water.

4. According to the World Resource Institute that "by the end of 2025, approximately 3.5 billion people - about half the world's population; will live in areas without enough water for agriculture, industry, and human needs globally. Furthermore, there are going to be a decrease in water quality in all regions including the one that have intensive agriculture, and large urban or industrial areas."

5. The two disadvantages of main rainwater harvesting are the predictability of rainfall and the responsibility of maintenance.

6. A well thought out maintenance schedule it can make rainwater harvesting easy and rewarding.

7. Rainwater harvesting has numerous advantages that make it superior to municipality provided water that are not limited to but water security, stainability, purity, inexpensive, simple to understand and easy to maintenance.

Chapter 1: Basic Components of Rainwater Harvesting Systems

Rainwater harvesting systems come in a variety of shapes and sizes depending on the physical area available from which to collect and store the rain as well as its intended use. While some of these systems collect rainwater directly, most collect off surfaces or rooftops.

Let's first perform a comparative analysis by examining the two separate paths a rain drop takes through a traditional centralized treatment facility verses an on-site rainwater harvesting system.

Traditional Centralized Treatment Facility - A Hard Path!

A centralized treatment facility consists of a large distribution/conveyance infrastructure of pumps, mains/laterals, treatment systems, storage reservoirs and extensive service delivery system.

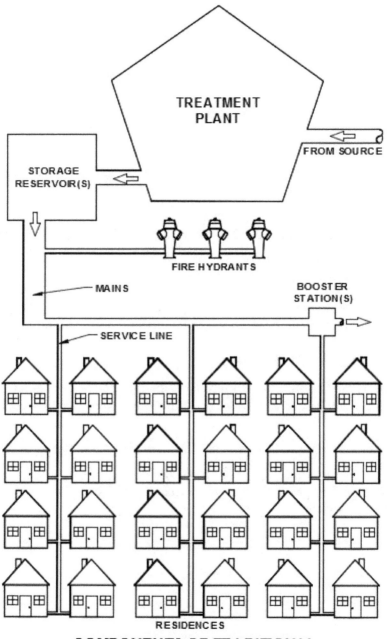

TREATMENT
PLANT

FROM SOURCE

STORAGE
RESERVOIR(S)

FIRE HYDRANTS

MAINS

BOOSTER
STATION(S)

SERVICE LINE

RESIDENCES

COMPONENTS OF TRADITIONAL
PUBLIC WATER SYSTEM

Once a raindrop hits the earth's surface it finds its way into one of the numerous sources that municipalities pull from to meet their customer's needs. Examples of these sources are manmade and natural reservoirs, lakes, rivers, wells and aquifers.

From the source, the raindrop is transferred into a reservoir(s) via the complex infrastructure of a municipal water system and eventually to their customers.

H_2O is a very effective solvent and it as ample opportunity in the complex maze of a public water system infrastructure to come into contact with a host of foreign contaminates and absorb their harmful constituents.

Common Harmful Constituents:
- Organic compounds
- Trash
- Animal waste
- Industrial waste
- Pharmaceuticals
- Oils
- Chemicals

It is truly amazing with all the opportunities for water to come into contact with so many pollutants in a public water system that there are not more incidences of contaminated water reaching end users.

One of the main ways the public water system combats delivering contaminated water to your house is via chemical treatment. There is much controversy around the chemical treatment of water, it's purity and its health impacts.

Additionally, there are justifiable concerns with the security, health and sustainability of public water systems as water sources diminish and the population grows.

Rainwater Harvesting - The Path of Least Resistance

Regardless of the purpose, use or types of water collected, all rainwater harvesting systems entail three main components. These components are **catchment surface, conveyance/delivery system and storage reservoirs.**

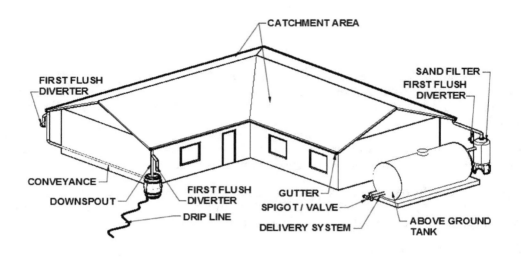

CATCHMENT AREA

FIRST FLUSH DIVERTER

SAND FILTER
FIRST FLUSH DIVERTER

CONVEYANCE

DOWNSPOUT

FIRST FLUSH DIVERTER

DRIP LINE

GUTTER

SPIGOT / VALVE

DELIVERY SYSTEM

ABOVE GROUND TANK

COMPONENTS OF A BASIC RAINWATER HARVESTING SYSTEM

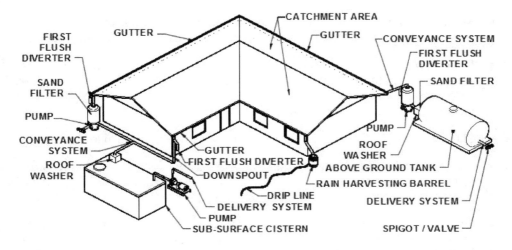

COMPONENTS OF A COMPLEX RAINWATER HARVESTING SYSTEM

As you can see even with a more complex rainwater harvesting system the advantages are numerous including but not limited to water security, stainability, purity, inexpensive, simple to understand and easy to maintenance.

The 3 Basic Components

Catchment Surface

In a rainwater harvesting system, water is collected on a catchment surface such as a rooftop or as surface water and then is transferred to the delivery system for distribution.

Although rainwater harvesting systems can include manmade and natural landscaped features as catchment surfaces, for purposes of simplicity I will be focusing on traditional residential roof catchment areas in my examples.

As far as the roofing material for water collection is concerned, there is no singular recommendation; therefore, many kinds of materials are appropriate. However, if you plan to use the water for drinking purposes (potable), the water will need to be filtered - which is covered in Chapter 5: How to Treat Water for Quality Assurance. You must also must ensure that the catchment surface of a potable system is completely clean and free containments.

Here are several catchment area materials listed in their order of preference based on "smoothness" or its ability to efficiently move water:

- Glass i.e. Solar panels: – They are expensive but are gaining popularity due to their dual purpose.

- Metal: Galvalume is a commonly used material for metal roofing which is a coated sheet metal that has a 55% to 45% aluminum to zinc alloy blend

- Concrete/Clay Tiles: A good, less expensive choice but as much as 10% loss can occur due to evaporation, porous surface texture and inefficient flow. Also caution must be taken to ensure that the porous surface has been treated with a non-toxic sealant.

- Slate: Smooth and excellent choice for potable use but it is also expensive.

- Composite shingles/Asphalt: Can also have a loss rate as high as 10% due to rough surface texture, inefficient flow and evaporation. The leaching of contaminates render this choice inappropriate choice for potable systems.

- Other: green roofs, gravel & wood. Although these types are not typical where they are used the leaching of contaminates also render these choices inappropriate for potable systems.

As we can see the best surface areas are smooth ones, such as glass and metal, which contribute minimal debris to the collected water. Asphalt and composite roofs are the worst offenders, as they not only contribute particulates from the material they are constructed from but also from the foreign objects that attach to their rough and irregular surfaces, which can then get transferred into the storage reservoir.

Additionally, the catchment area needs to be of sufficient size in order to collect adequate water for your needs. In some cases, when a site doesn't have a big enough catchment area a rain 'barn' or shed will be put up to increase catchment surface area. In Chapter 3: How to Design a Rainwater Harvesting System, I cover how to calculate your site's catchment area and determine if it's adequate enough for your water demand.

Conveyance/Delivery System

Rainwater collected from the catchment area needs to be transferred to the storage reservoir by the conveyance system, which is formed from gutters that attach at the edges of a roof leading to downspouts and terminate at the reservoir. The delivery system continues from the output side of the reservoir and can be as simple as a dripline or a header pipe with distribution pump(s). The number and size of the pumps needed depends on the amount of water you need and the height and/or distance you wish to move the water. Additionally, many systems include leaf screens, first flush diverters and roof washers, which are all covered in detail in Chapter 3: How to Design a Rainwater Harvesting System.

The delivery systems for potable designs also include filtration, treatment and purification which I cover in Chapter 5: How to Treat Water for Quality Assurance.

Typically, metal or plastic are used as the preferred material for this system. In order to ensure its proper functionality, the design of the guttering system is very important. Here are some pros and cons to considerate:

- Metal:
    - Pro: lasts longer/durable/seamless/aesthetically pleasing
    - Con: Cost more and can eventually rusts and can releases contaminates into the water
- Plastic:
    - Pro: Inexpensive/commonly used/easy to install/flexible
    - Con: Cracks/wears earlier/non-seamless (connections points can leak) and can be less aesthetically pleasing than metal

The gutters should have a slope of ½ inch (1.27 Centimeter) for every 10 feet (3 Meters) of linear gutter to guarantee sufficient water movement. If a you have a 20-foot gutter and one end has an elevation of 12 feet (12'-0") then the other end of the gutter run should have an elevation of 11 feet 6 inches (11'-6").

If the slope is too shallow, water may stagnate in the catchment area, which will not only contaminate all the collected water, but it will also become a breeding ground for mosquitos, flies and other unwanted pests. The following diagram illustrates the example given above.

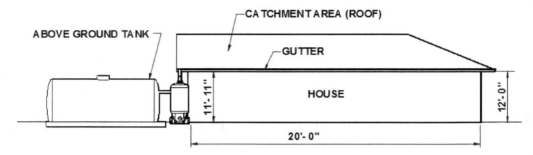

1/2" FOR EVERY 10'-0" OF LINEAR RUN OF GUTTER

GUTTER SLOPE

If you live in an area that experiences heavy, high-intensity rainfalls, then you can expect the rainwater to shoot over the gutters. This may lead to a reduction in collection so in order to address this issue, it is best to use a gutter splash/spill guard which are explained further in Chapter 3: How to Design a Rainwater Harvesting System.

As a rule of thumb a well-designed and efficient delivery system should be able to transfer as much as 75%+ of the water collected from the catchment area. If you absolutely need to know exactly how much water you are harvesting, measurement can be performed with residential flow meters that even come with remote monitoring options. Basically, if the catchment area is clean, completely free of debris, made from the recommended listed materials, with a clean, clog and leak free delivery system you will come as close to 75% as it you physically can get.

Storage Reservoirs

The water collected is stored at a specified location known as the storage reservoir. End users access the collected water from this storage reservoir via spigots/taps or valves and in some cases pumps. There are numerous components in a system, but the reservoir(s) is one of the most important and expensive components that needs to be carefully selected.

The size, capacity and strength of the storage reservoir depends heavily on your location, budget and water needs. With a clever design, you can accurately calculate the ideal size of reservoir you need to meet your water demands so that you don't, overbuilding and unnecessarily increasing your budget.

For instance, if you are implementing rainwater harvesting at a small scale, then you can conveniently use vessels such as barrels for storing the collected water. On the other hand, if you plan to store enough water to be used for most or all of your domestic needs, then you will need to install a tank below or above the ground. For domestic usages, tanks with capacities that range between 8,000 to 12,000 gallons (30 to 45+ cubic meters). However, for commercial purposes, tanks of higher capacities like 13,000 to 25,000+ gallons (50 to 100 cubic meters) are common.

A simple and quick calculation to properly size a reservoir looks like such:

- Catchment Area - A house that measures 40'x100' has a roof catchment area of 4000 Square feet.

- Annual Rain Fall - As an example Portland Oregon, the annual rain fall is 36".

- Loss - When calculating total catchment potential, a common multiplier of 0.46 is used to account for loss through evaporation and leaks.

Therefore, the equation is **4,000 x 36 x 0.46 = <u>66,240</u>** gallons annually.

A systems surge point (the highest rainfall in a season) is the most important element to include in your calculations when sizing a reservoir. To obtain this piece of information you can go to a site like this (http://average-rainfall.findthebest.com/l/201/Portland-Oregon) and obtain the inches from the month with the highest rainfall for your area.

For instance, in 2014, Portland received almost 7 inches by the end of December 2014. Thus, 10 inches would be a safe number to use in the calculation. Recalculate as such: 4,000 x 10 = 18,400 gallons.

At the highest rainfall (surge point), a home in Portland with a 4,000 square foot catchment area potentially could harvest 18,400 gallons of water in the month of December

Additionally, potential harvestable gallons projected for surge points often exceed the use demand. So, instead of installing a huge reservoir(s) that is only full a few months out of the year, I recommend that you go with a smaller reservoir(s) and use drip systems and/or surface holding ponds for irrigation/landscaping and/or smaller less expensive reservoirs like rain barrels.

We will go into detail on reservoirs in <u>Chapter 4: Everything about Storage Reservoirs</u>

Chapter Summary

1. Catchment Surface areas include rooftops, open surface water (ponds/tanks) and manmade/natural landscaped features.

2. Acceptable roofing materials for a catchment surface: Glass i.e. Solar panels, Metal, Concrete/Clay Tiles, Slate, Composite shingles/Asphalt, Other: green roofs, gravel & wood.

3. The smoother the material of the catchment area surface the more efficiently the water will be harvested.

4. You must keep the catchment surface of a potable system is kept clean and free containments.

5. A Conveyance system transfers the collected rainwater from the catchment area to the storage reservoir.

6. Conveyance systems are usually the guttering systems of a structure.

7. The delivery system continues from the output side of the reservoir usually

8. in the form of a dripline or a header pipe.

9. The delivery systems for potable designs also include filtration, treatment and purification.

10. Typically, metal or plastic are the materials used for the construction of conveyance and delivery systems.

11. Gutters should have a slope of ½ inch (1.27 Centimeter) for every 10 feet (3 Meters) of linear gutter to guarantee sufficient water movement.

12. If you plan to use the water for drinking purposes (potable), the water needs to be filtered.

13. Reservoirs are simply cisterns, barrels or tanks where collected rainwater is stored

14. Reservoir(s) are the most important and expensive components of a RWH system.

15. With a well-designed rainwater harvesting system you can accurately calculate the ideal size of reservoir you need to meet your water demands.

16. Domestic tanks have capacity ranges between 8,000 to 12,000 gallons (30 to 45+ cubic meters) and common commercial tanks have capacities between 13,000 to 25,000+ gallons (50 to 100 cubic meters)

17. A simple calculation to size a reservoir:
    Catchment Area (Square feet) x Your regions annual rainfall x 0.46 (Loss factor) = Annual Harvest Potential (gallons)

18. A systems surge point equals the highest rainfall in a season.

19. It is better to design a smaller simpler system that can be expanded rather than overbuilding a system that cost more and goes unused.

Chapter 2: Pre-requisites for Setting up a Rainwater Harvesting System

The correct installation and optimum efficiency of a system depends on many factors. Cost, climatic conditions, technical feasibility and financial factors play a crucial role in determining if rainwater harvesting will work for you. It also helps you choose the right type of rainwater harvesting system that will best meet your needs.

Environmental Factors

I know this may sound like a no brainer but the fundamental pre-requisite of rainwater harvesting is rainwater! You cannot harvest rainwater if it is a rarity in your region. Therefore, environmental factors are certainly the most-influential factors. The environmental feasibility of your rainwater harvesting can be decided by analyzing the following factors:

- Average rainfall in the region – as we discussed earlier in the storage reservoirs section
- Dry period duration – crucial information for designing a RWHS
- Other water sources – such as: rivers, creeks, ponds, lakes surface holding ponds, grey water

As a rule, rainwater harvesting is most feasible for regions that experience rainfall of 2 inches (50mm) per month for at least 6 months in a year.

The ideal climate for setting up a rainwater-harvesting project is a tropical climate, like Hawaii, Florida Puerto Rico and the Virgin Islands. Tropical climates have frequent and heavy rainfall with particularly short dry periods. Therefore, the water collected during the wet period can be conveniently used during the dry spells. In addition, a state like Oregon has a west coast but desert in the central and east regions which are also an excellent candidate for RWH.

Technical Factors

The second most-important consideration for a rainwater-harvesting project is technical feasibility. The following factors need to be addressed before taking the plunge:

- In order to install the system's storage reservoir, you must have at least 3 – 6 feet (1 to 2 m) of available area on site.

- Your roofing must be made of tile, metal, concrete, asphalt or composite shingle, see section on catchment areas.

There are several additional factors that have to be considered regarding the size and capacity for a rainwater-harvesting project, such as:

- Number of users

- Water consumption/usage

- Availability of alternate sources

- Availability of materials and skilled labor

Usage and consumption are the two most important technical factors. Typically, four kinds of usage patterns exist:

- **Occasional**
  Most areas may experience regular rainfalls. However, there may be intermittent dry periods that may last only a few days. An alternative source of water can be used such as smaller reservoirs for occasional consumption.

- **Intermittent**
  In areas where long rain-periods are separated by dry spells, stored water is used to suffice water demands during these spells.

- **Partial**
  In this case, rainwater harvested is used for the entire year. Therefore, harvested water is not the only source of water; an alternate source is also used.

- **Full**
  Harvested rainwater is the only source of supply water. Therefore, management of water and a clever choice of the storage reservoir are necessary to ensure that you sail through the dry spell with ease.

As far as user consumption is concerned, an individual can use as much as 100 gallons (375+ liters) of water per day. The per-user consumption of water depends on a number of factors, but climate is the most significant one. Aside that, socio-economic status and education level of the individuals also determine the amount of water he or she uses and wastes.

The other two factors, which play an important role in determining the feasibility of your domestic rainwater-harvesting project, are budget and availability of materials and labor. Review the following listed essential materials below to ensure that you have all the necessary resources:

- The roofing or catchment area needs to be made of the materials listed in Chapter 1.

- Gutter and delivery system with constructions of metal or PVC is commonly used.

- Common construction of storage reservoir includes; brick & mortar, re-enforced concrete, fiberglass, metal, or plastic.

- Depending on reservoir and system complexity type you will need either a tap/spigot or a pump for removing water from the storage reservoir.

Financial Factors

Budget is certainly one of the dominating factors when it comes to making decisions regarding installation. The storage reservoir will be the most expensive thing on your budget and rainwater-harvesting project will require an investment in quality materials and quality workmanship to construct it.

In the majority of cases, a roof will function perfectly as appropriate catchment surface. Furthermore, you can use existing guttering assembly, downspouts and a barrel to save cost. However, if you are looking for more sophisticated system, it will obviously be more expensive.

Chapter Summary

1. Important factors that need to be considered for the installation of an efficient RWH system include cost, climatic conditions, technical feasibility and financial factors.

2. Environmental factors include; Average rainfall in the region, dry period duration and other water sources.

3. Technical factors include; Available space 3 – 6 feet (1 to 2 m), appropriate catchment material, number of users, water consumption/usage, availability of alternate sources and availability of materials and skilled labor

4. Financial factors include; Simple systems are usually extremely affordable (Under $100) and complex systems can cost thousands of dollars.

5. Is Rainwater Harvesting for you? Here is a list of questions to answer before deciding on which type of rainwater-harvesting system to install on your site:

   - Is rainwater harvesting environmentally feasible?

     o What is the average rainfall rate and pattern in your region?

     o Are other sources of water available?

   - Is rainwater harvesting technically feasible?

- Do you have enough area for the catchment surface?
- What is the water consumption of your family?
- What is the usage pattern of your family?
- What is the run-off coefficient (material and slope)?

Chapter 3: How to Design a Rainwater Harvesting System

In designing a rainwater-harvesting system, the most-crucial consideration is to ensure that you have chosen the right size and type of storage reservoir that will meet your water consumption needs. The designing of a Rainwater Harvesting System has a four-step process, which I describe in detail, in this chapter.

Step 1: Analyze the Requirements

Before setting up any system, it is imperative that you list out your requirements. As part of the requirements, you need to state the following:

1. Water Demand

   You can decide upon the scale and complexity of the project only after you know your family's water demands. You can estimate your approximate yearly water consumption by simply multiplying your average daily water use with the number of members in the household and then multiply the sum by **365** (Days in a year). According to the United States Geological Survey (United States Department of the Interior) the average daily consumption of a Westerner is between 80-100 gallons (300-380L)/day. Since it is impossible to know specifically what the reader's daily consumption is we will use the average mean of **90** gallons (340L)/day for our example:

   If the average daily water consumption of one person is 90 gallons and there are **4** people in a household, then water demand is given by:

   Annual Water Demand = **90*4*365 = 131,400 gallons/annually.**

   Please note that you need to use the average daily consumption value. Since daily consumption values vary from person to person and season to season absolute values cannot be used. Additionally, water consumption is not just limited to personal use. There are several other factors that determine usage such as fixture type (low flow vs. high flow), irrigation needs, pools/spas, cleaning, laundry and other household chores. Therefore, these parameters should be kept in mind when calculating the average daily per-person water consumption.

2. Climatic Conditions

   It is crucial to obtain the amount of average rainfall in your area. If you live in an arid region, then installing a high capacity, complex rainwater harvesting system would be overspending, because it could take years to fill and only days/weeks to drain it dry. Therefore, it is crucial for you to obtain the average rainfall and household consumption to determine the size of the system. In addition, it will allow you to estimate the amount of water that is available for you to collect. Thus, collecting data about your local climatic condition is the first step towards designing your system.

As part of your data collection, you must collect information about both the monthly as well as yearly rainfall in your area. For instance, if the average monthly rainfall is regular – between 2 and 6 inch a month; then you do not need a high capacity storage reservoir. Specific and comprehensive analysis of climate data can add valuable detailing to your design and reduce cost.

An excellent source for finding the rainfall average for your area you can go here: http://www.worldclimate.com/

3. Catchment Area

    The catchment area can be defined as the area available from which to harvest rainwater from, such as a roof.   This can be calculated by multiplying the square footage of the catchment area times the average rainfall times 0.46 to determine potential rainwater that is harvestable. The variable of 0.46 is used to represent the average amount of water lost due to loss through evaporation and leaks.

    As an example, a building that is 50'-0" by 60'-0" has a roof with a catchment area of approximately 3,000 square feet.

    In a location with an average rainfall of 30 inches per year the calculation would be as follows: **3,000*30*0.46=41,400 gallons in annual capture potential.**

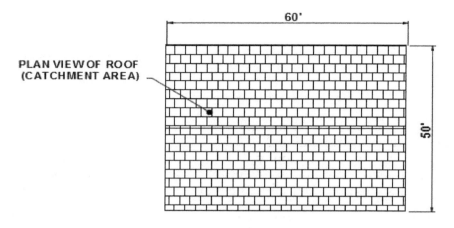

1. CATCHMENT AREA (60'-0" x 50'-0") = 3,000 SQUARE FEET
2. REGION WITH AN AVERAGE ANNUAL RAINFALL OF 30 INCHES PER YEAR
3. MULTIPLIER OF 0.46 FOR LOSS DUE TO EVAPORATION AND LEAKS

CALCULATION: 3,000 x 30 x 0.46 = 41,400 GALLONS IN ANNUAL CAPTURE POTENTIAL

CAPTURE POTENTIAL

Step 2: Design Catchment Area

The most commonly used option for a catchment area is the rooftop. However, the roof should be regularly cleaned if you wish to use it for domestic purposes. It is also important to consider the material that the catchment area is constructed from. Ideally, the roof should be constructed out of the materials out lined in Chapter 1. In addition, flat cement surfaces and thatched roofs are also considered good for rainwater harvesting purposes. Therefore, if you have a rooftop that is water resistant and/or is capable of holding water, you have a free catchment area ready for your use.

Other important considerations for rainwater harvesting are the area available for catchment and run-off coefficient. Typically, the run-off coefficient should be at least .75, meaning your roof must allow run-off of 75% of the water that is collected on it. Galvanized metal provides the best run-off coefficients; thatched roofs have the lowest value for this parameter.

Material	Run-Off Coefficient
Asphalt	0.9
Galvanized	0.85
Concrete	0.85
Tile (Terra Cotta)	0.07

Aluminum	0.9
Wood	0.65

Step 3: Design Conveyance/Delivery System

The most-common type of conveyance system used for rainwater harvesting is a guttering system. Typically, the delivery system consists of the drip line, hose or piping you choose to use to deliver the water to its intended use.

Conveyance and delivery components include in addition to gutters; splash guards, leaf screens, leaf guards, first flush diverters, roof washers, pump(s) and in the case of potable systems, final filtration.

Gutter Systems

As part of this system, gutters need to be attached at the ends of the catchment area and downspouts need to be installed, which carry water from the catchment area to the storage area. The gutter downspouts that are attached to the gutter drop outlets should have clean tight connection points to mitigate leaks. A common downspout arrangement to attach two 45° elbow together which allows the assembly to be securely attached to the structure to give the assembly strength and rigidly. Additionally, the downspouts need to be numerous enough (At least one downspout every 20'-0") and large enough to effectively transfer the water to the reservoir and prevent overflow of the gutters. Generally, PVC or galvanized metal pipes are used for the construction of this kind of assembly.

There are several types of gutters that are available on the market. You can choose gutters made from sheet metal or pre-fabricated plastic. If you choose to use plastic gutters, they tend to be the most inexpensive option available. As a precaution, gutters made from PVC age and crack more readily due to direct sunlight; however, they are perfect for installation under roof areas. In addition, gutters are available in different shapes. Commonly available gutters are of Semi or Half Circle, "U"-Shaped, Rectangular, Trapezoidal and V-shaped.

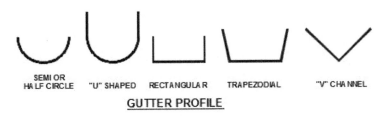

SEMI OR
HALF CIRCLE   "U" SHAPED   RECTANGULAR   TRAPEZODIAL   "V" CHANNEL
GUTTER PROFILE

We are concerned with a few factors when selecting shape:

P = Perimeter

W = Depth

A = Area

D3 = Stiffness

Interception efficiency, flow capacity and stiffness are attainable by three dimensionless ratios:

A/P^2 = Area Ratio

W/P = Aperture Ratio

D_3/P_3 = Stiffness Ratio

Gutter Shape	Area Ratio	Aperture Ratio	Stiffness Ratio
Semi-Circle	$A/P^2 = 0.159$	$W/P = 0.64$	$D^3/P^3 = 0.032$
"U" Shape	$A/P^2 = 0.135$	$W/P = 0.39$	$D^3/P^3 = 0.059$
Rectangular	$A/P^2 = 0.125$	$W/P = 0.50$	$D^3/P^3 = 0.016$
Trapezoidal	$A/P^2 = 0.134$	$W/P = 0.80$	$D^3/P^3 = 0.013$
"V" Shaped	$A/P^2 = 0.124$	$W/P = 0.71$	$D^3/P^3 = 0.044$

- For good interception, we require a big gutter aperture W.
- For high flow capacity, the area A should be as large as possible
- Stiffness D3 should be maximized

Don't get too bogged down in the math the important take away here is the higher the values, the better.

Commonly used options include:

- A suitable alternative is aluminum, which is a strong and anti-corrosive material.

- If you are looking for cheaper options, then you can also consider structures made from bamboo and planks of wood. However, these gutters are not durable and due to the presence of bacteria in these organic materials, the quality of water collected may also be sub-standard and unfit for use.

- Another cost-effective alternative for guttering is half pipes. The constructs are highly efficient because of their semi-circular shapes. They are also relatively easy to create for the do-it-yourself types.

Once you have decided on the type of gutter you wish to install, you need to ensure that the construction of the gutters is done as per the required standards for rainwater harvesting. Few things that you must consider include:

- You must confirm that the structure the gutters are attached to can support the weight of the system when it is full of rainwater.

- Gutters should slope appropriately towards the storage reservoir to allow easy drainage of water; a good rule of thumb is 1/8" (.635 cm) drop for every liner foot or ½" (1.27 cm) for every 10'-0" (3m) of liner run of gutter. If your gutter isn't draining properly you don't have enough slope.

- The downspouts used at the end of the gutters must be capable of carrying a minimum of 90% of the collected water.

- Areas that experience heavy rainfall should install splash guards to maximize efficient water collection into their delivery systems. A **splash guard** is an approximately 12 - 16 inch (30 cm) long strip of sheet metal that is installed in the gutter at the bottom of a roofs valley and acts as a barrier to keep the rainwater from shooting over the gutter.

It is important to recognize that a well-designed gutter system can play a crucial role in increasing the life of your home. It allows your walls to remain dry and prevents erosion of your homes foundation.

Leaf Screens & Leaf Guards

A leaf screen or leaf guard are simply a screen, mesh or perforated metal insert which covers the top surface of the gutter to filters out debris washed down from the catchment area. Screens are typically used to filter out larger debris and guards are used for high concentration of debris; both are excellent first stage filtration components for a rainwater harvesting system.

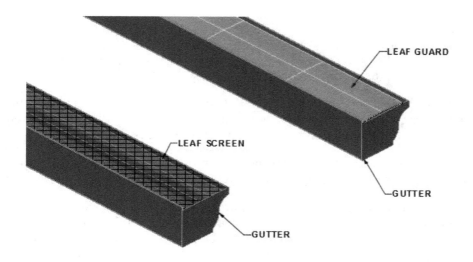

EXAMPLES OF A LEAF SCREEN & A LEAF GUARD

Strainer Baskets

Strainer baskets are very simple tapered spherical basket with sides made of mesh or screen and fit down into the downspout through the gutters drop outlet. Strainers act as a first or second stage filtration for a rainwater harvesting system but must be cleaned out on a regular basis to prevent overflow due to plugging by debris.

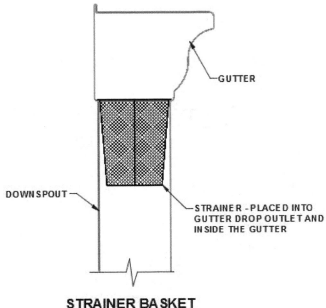

GUTTER

DOWNSPOUT

STRAINER - PLACED INTO GUTTER DROP OUTLET AND INSIDE THE GUTTER

STRAINER BASKET

First Flush Diverter

First-flush devices and techniques are used to divert the rainwater collected from first rainfall from entering the storage reservoir. Although, this device is not a mandatory component of the system, its use is recommended for improved water quality.

Commonly one of the following three methods is used for diverting the first-flush. These methods are:

1. The first of these methods is the fixed volume method. In this case, a fixed volume container is used for collecting the first-flush and once the water is collected, this container is drained out.

2. The second method is a manual method in which the down-pipe is removed from the inlet of the reservoir and the water is automatically diverted away.

3. Roof washer with valve and divert tee. A simple rule of thumb to follow for how much water is sufficient for a first flush is 10 gallons for every 1,000 square feet of catchment area. However, you will need to use your own judgement as to if additional gallons are required to properly wash your catchment area. This is especially true if you live in an area that is subject to higher than normal amounts of debris that accumulate on your catchment area from trees and/other sources.

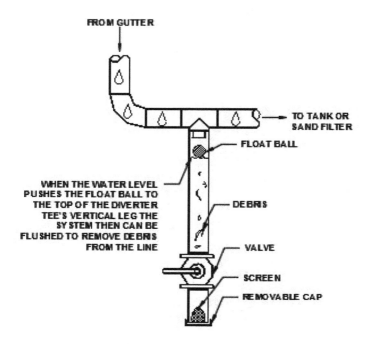

FROM GUTTER

TO TANK OR
SAND FILTER

FLOAT BALL

WHEN THE WATER LEVEL
PUSHES THE FLOAT BALL TO
THE TOP OF THE DIVERTER
TEE'S VERTICAL LEG THE
SYSTEM THEN CAN BE
FLUSHED TO REMOVE DEBRIS
FROM THE LINE

DEBRIS

VALVE

SCREEN

REMOVABLE CAP

ROOF WASHER DIVERTER TEE

Roof Washers

A roof washer is recommended for potable systems and ideal for systems that use distribution drip lines and/or smaller diameter distribution/conveyance piping that can clog easily. Roof washers are designed to remove smaller debris that get past leaf gourds/screens, basket strainers and first flush diverters.

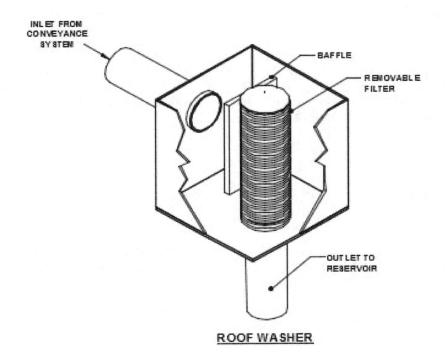

INLET FROM
CONVEYANCE
SYSTEM

BAFFLE

REMOVABLE
FILTER

OUTLET TO
RESERVOIR

ROOF WASHER

Pumps and Final Filtration

We will be covering pumps in Chapter 4: Everything about Storage Reservoirs and final filtration in Chapter 5: How to Treat Water for Quality Assurance.

Step 4: Designing a Storage Reservoir

Now that you have the catchment area and delivery system ready, the final component of the rainwater harvesting system is the storage reservoir. Storage reservoirs are available in several different sizes and shapes. However, in order to choose the reservoir that best suits your needs, you can use one of the approaches explained below.

The first approach is called the *demand side* approach. It is the most widely accepted approach and is also the simplest method available.

This method uses the number of occupants and the required water volume; it is the best method to follow if you are living in a dry area. Using this method, the storage capacity required is calculated as such:

Required Storage Capacity = (Demand * Number of dry months) / 12

Where Demand = Per-day Per-person Water Consumption * Number of household members * 365

The demand side approach is a simple method that gives you a rough estimate on the required storage capacity. However, it does not take into account certain factors like drought years and assumes that there is sufficient catchment area and annual rainfall.

The second approach is called the _supply side_ approach and it is based on the average rainfall in your area. This method aims to maximize supply and is known to give a good assessment of your storage needs. The steps that you need to follow for this method are as follows:

Supply = R * A * Cr

Where:

R = Mean Annual Rain Fall (Averaged total amount of rain fall in a year)

A = Catchment Area in Square Feet

Cr = Coefficient of runoff. Cr is defined as the ratio of the volume of water that runs off the catchment area to the volume of rain that falls in a region, i.e. galvanized iron roofing has a high Cr of 0.9.

Once you are clear about the required storage capacity, you will need to choose the optimal design for your storage reservoir. The next Chapter will give you a detailed look at this facet of rainwater harvesting.

Chapter Summary
The 4 Steps to Designing a Rainwater Harvesting

1. **Step 1: Analyze the Requirements**

   - Water Demand formula:
     (Average daily water use x **Number of members in the household**) x **365 Days in a year** = **Your Demand**

   - Climatic Conditions - To obtain the amount of average rainfall in your area you can go here: http://www.worldclimate.com/

   - Catchment Area formula:
     Catchment Area (Square feet) x **Your regions annual rainfall** x **0.46 (Loss factor)** = **Annual Harvest Potential (gallons)**

2. **Step 2: Design Catchment Area**
   - The most commonly used area is the rooftop.
   - Common material: Asphalt, metal concrete, tile, aluminum
   - The run-off coefficient should be at least .75

3. **Step 3: Design Conveyance/Delivery System**

- Conveyance and Delivery systems can include:
- Gutter systems
- Splash guards
- Leaf screens/guards
- First flush diverters
- Roof washers
- Pump
- Final filtration (Potable systems)

4. **Step 4: Designing a Storage Reservoir**
   - Demand side formula: **Required Storage Capacity** = **(Demand * Number of dry months) / 12**
   - Supply side formula: **Required Storage Capacity** = **Averaged total amount of rain fall in a year** x **Catchment Area in Square Feet** x **Coefficient of runoff.**

Chapter 4: Everything about Storage Reservoirs

Storage reservoirs are by far the most-expensive components of a rainwater harvesting system and therefore need to be selected carefully.

Factors to Consider When Designing a Storage Reservoir?

Here are the crucial factors to consider when deciding on the reservoir size and type:

- Do you require a full, partial, intermittent or occasional rainwater harvesting system See Chapter 2 Environmental Factors
- Water requirements. See Chapter 1 - Step 1: Analyze the Requirements
- Budget
- Available space, Construction material & Shape
- Ground soil type and conditions
- Budget
- Skilled labor for installation
- Other sources of water storage

Budget

It is extremely difficult to give current and actuate costs for the varying components of a rainwater system since prices can vary widely depending on where you live and what kind of components you purchase. My recommendation is that you plan on spending 50-75% of your budget on your reservoir. The reservoir is the most expensive and important part of your system so it's a sensible idea to purchase the highest quality you can, the other components of the system are far less expensive to upgrade later.

Location, Construction Material & Shape

In the last step of the previous Chapter, we discussed how to calculate the required storage capacity of a reservoir. You will need that information for selecting your reservoir.

Location

As mentioned in Chapter 2 - Technical Factors, the minimum space required for a simple storage reservoir, will need at least 3 – 6 feet (1 to 2 m) of available area on site. Additionally, the reservoir should be located as close to supply and demand points of the conveyance/delivery systems. This will reduce exposure to sunlight and loss through evaporation and leakage.

If your environmental factors allow you to prudently go with a larger system, including filtration and/or an above ground tank then the footprint of those components dictate the amount of space required. Typically, the reservoir, especially an above ground one, will be the system component that requires the greatest real-estate footprint. Once you obtain your water demand and harvest potential you will then be able to use those metrics to determine the size of your reservoirs footprint.

Sub-surface tanks are installed below the surface of the ground and can have serval challenges, thus, you need to consider several things during designing a sub-surface tank, such as:

- The tank must be able to withstand the pressure of the surrounding ground, particularly when it is full.

- Landscaping; the tank needs to be located in a spot that is free of possible infiltration of tree roots.

- All underground takes should be located a minimum of 50' away from animal stables/barns and/or surface waste water holding ponds.

- The height of installation must be carefully considered as well. The tank should be well above the ground water level. Also, you must keep a section of the tank above surface level or install a port for access and servicing. The ground water below the level of foundations can wick upward through the soil by capillary action and in very fine soils, this capillary rise can be as much as 8 feet. The major point here is, the necessity of setting a foundation or stand for the above ground tanks in order to avoid having issues with ground water levels. In addition, you also need to allow enough room between the bottom spigot assembly and the ground for further maintenance.

- Water has great weight and therefore a tank foundation needs to be laid. The soil should first be compacted with a layer sand and pea gravel. In hard stable soil this may be sufficient for some tanks but pouring a concrete pad is highly recommended. If you have any doubts about your soil or tank, I recommend you enlist the help of a structural engineer or architect.

Construction Material

The next step is to select the construction material for your reservoir. I always encourage people to select what fits easily into their budget and is easily found in their area. Start small and if you have to expand your system later, you can do so.

A quick note about the color of the tank. If you plan on installing an above ground tank it's important that it's opaque to inhibit algae growth. Painting or covering a tank would be another acceptable options.

Storage reservoirs can be placed above or below ground, but they have differing characteristics depending on their placement.

Surface tanks or the tanks that are placed above ground are mostly used for rooftop water collection. These tanks are available in a range of materials for you to choose from:

- **Plastic (Food grade):** 50-100 gallons, cylinder shaped (Rain Barrel), good for surface or sub surface installation, easy to repair, inexpensive

- **Ceramic Clay or Stone:** 50-100 gallons, cylinder shaped (Rain Barrel), good for surface or sub surface installation, easy to repair, inexpensive

- **Ferrocement:** – Size can vary greatly due to countless shapes and sizes from site poured installation, good for surface installation, weathers well, prone to cracking, easy to repair, inexpensive

- Concrete: Size can vary greatly due to countless shapes and sizes from site poured installation. Prefabricated tanks are also available for site delivery, good for surface or sub surface installation, weathers well, prone to cracking, inconvenient to repair, expensive

- **Metal:** 150-2,500 gallons – typically cylinder shaped, good for surface installation, needs painting to extend life, easy to repair, inexpensive to expensive

- **Wood:** 500-35,00 gallons, typically cylinder/round shaped, good for surface installation, weathers well, portable, easy to repair, inexpensive to expensive.

- **Polypropylene:** 50-10,000 Gallons, typically cylinder/round shaped, good for surface installation, weathers well, inexpensive

- **Fiberglass:** 50-15,00 gallons, typically cylinder shaped, good for surface or sub surface installation, weathers well, easy to repair, integral parts reduce leakage, expensive

Sub-surface tanks are usually made from concrete, fiberglass or reinforced food grade plastic. In order to extract water from these tanks, you will need a pump or a rope and bucket - for an inexpensive alternative; similar to that used for pulling water from a well. Whether surface or sub-surface all tanks require filtration and regular maintenance to prevent water contamination.

Surface tanks are more durable whereas sub-surface tanks are more cost-effective. Therefore, the tank you choose depends upon your preference, space available and budget.

Shape

Once you have finalized the material to be used for construction, you must choose a shape that is appropriate for the chosen material. In most cases, a cylindrical shape is chosen. In addition, round shaped reservoirs are also a variety of shapes manufactured especially for commercial and industrial uses.

In addition to a capacity-based classification, storage reservoirs are also classified on the basis of their shape and location of installation. Generally, storage reservoirs are available in rectangle, square or round/sphere shapes. Round/sphere shaped tanks are popular because of their increased strength and minimum maintenance requirements.

Above ground cisterns can be of any shape to fit space available. Round is recommended for strength and easy to clean, no corners. A buried cistern needs to be strong enough to resist being crushed by the surrounding earth especially when empty. Particular shapes/materials are designed for this, such as concrete that can be made for any shape but requires thick walls or plastic that are made with deeply ribbed spheres and usually elongated.

Examples of Tanks

300 – 10,000 Gallon Round Above Ground Cisterns

Gallon Underground Sphere Cistern

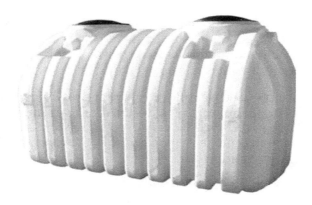

1200 Gallon Underground Cistern

900 & 1,800 Gallon Underground Precast Concrete Cisterns

Water Extraction Devices

Now that the water has been collected and is in the storage reservoir, you need an easy way to extract the water from the tank. Common extraction devices include:

- Spigot/Taps

  This simple method is done with a spigot similar to a hose bib placed 6"-24" (depending on size of the tank) from the bottom of the tank and gravity does the work. All surface tanks can be purchased with this option.

- Pressure Tanks and Water Pumps

  If your storage reservoir is sub-surface, then you will need a device for extracting water from the tank, the most-appropriate option in most cases is a water pump. The pumps required for residential application are usually of smaller HP and are easy to install. Once you have determined the specifics of your systems requirements any competent pump manufactures representative should easily be able to assist you in selecting the right sized pump for your system. Additionally, solar pumps are a great option to consider for most rainwater harvesting installations.

  If, however you plan to use your rainwater for household chores you will need to bring the water pressure (psi) in the system up to the psi needs of the appliances in your home. Municipal water sources have a range of 40-60 psi and household appliances have a psi demand between 20-30 psi.

  To raise the water pressure in your system using the pump and pressure tank method the pump simply pulls water from the reservoir and into a pressure tank until it is needed. Typically pressure tanks are 40 gallons and are set to auto-fill via the tanks pressure switch. A check valve gives the system backflow prevention keeping the water from returning to the tank.

- On-Demand Pump

  This method eliminates the need for a pressure tank as the pumps are all in-one self-priming and have incorporated check valves. They are usually easy plug and play type installations – connect and flip the switch. A typical installation of an on-demand pump includes a 5-microm fiber filter, 3-micron activated charcoal filter, and an ultra-violent lamp.

Dealing with Tank Overflow

In addition to the above-mentioned it is important that both surface and sub-surface tanks include an overflow management device. Usually, an over-flow pipe is installed at the mouth of the tank and as soon as the water level rises beyond a preset level, the water is redirected to another storage location, such as a surface holding pond or a smaller reservoir like a rain barrel.

Chapter Summary

1. Choose whether you want to install a sub-surface or surface reservoir.

2. Choose the material that is available to you and is well within your budget.

3. The tank should be created at such a location that it is easily accessible.

4. If you are planning to construct a surface tank, then you must ensure that the foundation is strong enough to support the construct. On the other hand, if you wish to get a sub-surface tank constructed, you must ensure that the soil is stable.

5. If you live in an area that experiences seasonal flooding, then you must construct the sub-surface tank on higher ground level.

6. The tank must be created at such a location that it stays away from direct sunlight or exposure to debris and other sources of contamination.

7. While designing the storage reservoir and delivery system, it must be ensured that the downspout-pipe is located at the lowest point of the catchment area.

8. It is important to ensure that the construction is strong and easily accessible for cleaning however it should be secure from unwanted persons or animals.

9. A tapping device, such as a spigot must be installed.

10. You will need to use a pressure tank/pump or on-demand pump to raise the water pressure in your system if you plan to use the water with household appliances

11. All measures must be taken to ensure that the quality of water is maintained. See Chapter 5.

12. In order to avoid any damage to the construct and its foundation, it is important to install appropriate overflow devices.

13. Appropriate slopes must be created from the delivery system to the tank to ensure efficient water flow.

14. You will need to use a pressure tank/pump or on-demand pump to raise the water pressure in your system if you plan to use the water with household appliances

15. You must ensure that the system is maintained well. See Chapter 6.

Chapter 5: Water Quality Assurance

If you are intending to use the harvested rainwater for domestic purposes like cooking and bathing, this is where water quality becomes immensely important. This chapter introduces the different techniques and devices that must be used for maintaining the quality of water.

IMPORTANT: It is imperative that you must check the building/plumbing code in your area to ascertain whether or not harvesting rainwater for domestic use is allowed and legal.

How to Avoid Degradation of Water Quality?

- If you are living in a highly industrial area, you must be sure the rainwater collected is from a well-maintained catchment area and is safe for human use. This is a common maintenance item that many people overlook, your roof needs at least cleaning once a year possibly more often depending on the location.

- Never use the rainwater collected from the first heavy rainfalls instead use this water for maintenance of the system. A roof washer diverter tee installed in the downspouts allows the gutters to be flushed separately by diverting away the debris filled gutter water and keeps it from contaminating the rest of the system. The water is diverted via a simple valve and pipe to a holding pond, secondary container or French drain.

- Once the gutters have been thoroughly flushed additional first rains should be used to flush the entire deliver system. Disconnect the inlet pipe to the reservoir (The water should be diverted into a holding pond, secondary container or French drain), set the valve on the diverter tee to feed the water into the system and let nature do the work.

- Dirt settles at the base of the tank, therefore the tap installed in the tank must be placed 4-6 inches (10-15 cm) above the base of the tank. However, if you wish to use the water for drinking purposes, then you must place the tap at least 20 inches (50 cm) above the tank base.

- You can ensure optimum quality by choosing the right design and maintaining the system well. The water quality can be further improved by using filters or flush devices. In addition, treatment methods like chlorination and UV treatment can also be used.

Basket Strainers, First Flush Diverters & Roof Washers

In Chapter 3: Step 3 - Designing a Conveyance /Delivery System we already covered these components in detail but I just wanted to mention them again to emphasize their importance as the first line of defense in keeping your water clean.

Filters

- Slow Sand Filters

  This kind of filter is particularly good for removing petroleum hydrocarbons that are released from traditional composition shingle type roofs but they also do an excellent job of removing containments from most types of catchment areas. The filter is a barrel that is filled half way with sand and is installed at the inlet of the tank. The rainwater fills the barrel and slowly trickles through the sand making the rainwater suitable for human consumption as it exits the filter at the bottom. A microbial layer forms above the sand which "eats" the biological impurities in the water and this microbial layer needs to be drained off occasionally and should NEVER be consumed by humans or animals.

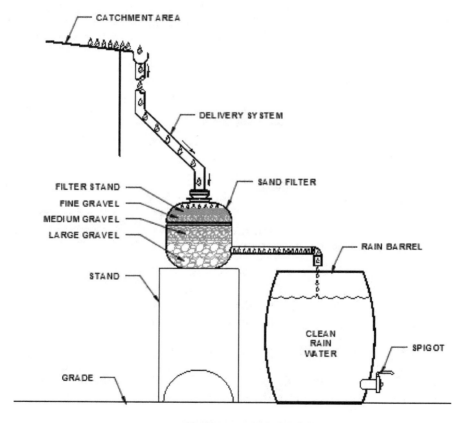

IN-LINE SAND FILTER

- Cartridge Filters as mentioned in <u>Chapter 4 Section: Water Extraction Devices</u> a common installation of cartridge filters includes a 5-microm fiber filter and a 3-micron activated charcoal filter. These kind of in-line filters are typically

- Ultraviolet Light (UV)

  A UV lamp is designed for the purification of potable water sources of microbiological contamination by disabling their reproductive process with high doses of ultra violet light energy. UV is a great alternative to using environmentally harmful chemicals.

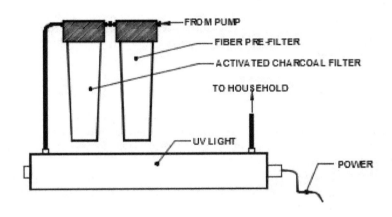

CARTRIDGE FILTERS AND ULTRAVIOLET LIGHT (UV)

Although filtration cartridges and UV lamps are one of the most common ways to purify rainwater there are also others options to consider as well:

- Purification tablets and backpacking membrane filters – Both of these solutions are used by backpackers and campers. They are designed for small amounts of water and are not meant for long term use. However, both or either of these items are excellent resources to have on hand in the case of an emergency. You can purchase both at most outdoor stores

- Boiling

  Boiling water is known to kill bacteria and microorganisms. However, it flattens the taste and is inconvenient.

- Sunlight

Sunlight is a natural disinfectant but it takes between 6-8 hours to work, only kills microbial pathogens and does not work on chemical toxins.

- Chlorination

  It must be noted that even though chlorination is a method of water purification, an excess of it can affect the taste of water and may lead to health issues. For the first dose, 3 tablespoons (40 ml) of Sodium Hypochlorite can be added to 265 gallons (1000 liters) of water. After initial stirring, the water should be left to stand for a day. You can use a color comparator kit available at most hardware stores to test for ensuring that the right amount of chlorine has been added. Please note that stabilized chlorine must not be used for water purification.

- Reverse Osmosis & Nanofiltration

  This kind of filtration uses high pressure to push water through semi-permeable membrane filters. There is lost due to "brine" water rejection from the system.

- Ozone purification systems

  Ozone is created by the sun's ultra violet rays that react with our upper atmosphere which makes up the Earth's protective ozone layer. Ozone can be produced in what's called an Ozone Generator. It's a compressed air chamber containing a high intensity Ultraviolet (UV) lamp that converts oxygen into ozone. The ozone is then drawn through a diffuser creating ozone saturated bubbles which are mixed with the water and then held in a purification tank.

Chapter Summary

16. IMPORTANT: It is imperative that you must check the building/plumbing code in your area to ascertain whether or not harvesting rainwater for domestic use is allowed and legal.

17. The catchment surface should not be coated with any toxic material and it should be sterilized bi-annually.

18. Never use the rainwater collected from the first heavy rainfalls.

19. Taps installed in a tank must be placed 4-6 inches (10-15 cm) for general use and at least 20 inches (50 cm) above the base of the tank.

20. Filtration and purification systems; Slow Sand Filters, Cartridge Filters, Ultraviolet Light (UV), Reverse Osmosis, & Nanofiltration and Ozone Purification Systems.

Chapter 6: Maintaining a Rainwater Harvesting Systems

Maintenance is usually the most-neglected facet of a systems use and like many other systems in your home is maintenance crucial for optimal performance.

Maintenance tasks can be divided into two categories, periodic tasks and annual tasks, and entail the maintenance of the catchment area, delivery system and storage reservoirs.

Periodic Maintenance Checklist

1. The gutters and catchment area should be kept clean. It should be regularly washed and cleaned to avoid the presence of birds' droppings, leaves and other miscellaneous debris.

2. The filters should be cleaned on a regular basis.

3. Periodic cleaning of the mosquito screening should also be done.

4. During the dry periods, the inflow pipe should be disconnected from the reservoir. The pipe must be placed back in only after the system has been flushed and cleaned.

5. The system should be regularly checked for leakage. For instance, you can check the water level in the storage reservoir using a yardstick. If the water level is below your expected value, you can consider the possibility of a leak in the system.

Annual and Infrequent Tasks Checklist

1. If you have noticed any leaks in the system, you must plan a repair of the same as soon as possible.

2. Any breakages, wear, cracks and tears must be addressed immediately.

3. All the filters installed in the system must be regularly cleaned or replaced, on an as needed basis.

4. The tank must be emptied completely and cleaned on an annual basis.

5. If repairs have been made, the system should be scrubbed using cleaning solution and then let stand for 1 ½ days after which the entire system should be flushed with clean water. A simple cleaning solution can be made by: using one of the following methods:

   o Adding 1-part water to 3 parts vinegar
   o Adding 1-part baking powder to 9 parts water

Treading Water...

Rainwater harvesting is no doubt one of the most useful and easy to implement tools we must help prevent the next urban water crisis.

Potable safe water is becoming a rare resource. No matter how much we try to save water in our homes, we still depend heavily on it in so many other aspects of our daily lives. There is rising pressure to find alternative supplies of clean, safe water and rainwater harvesting is one of the best options available.

You can implement it at the home level and scale up the design depending upon your requirements and budget. In this sense, a rainwater harvesting system offers you immense flexibility. Try out the design steps and advice given in this book and enjoy the benefits of a well-designed water harvesting system.

Finally, if you enjoyed this book, please take the time to share your thoughts and post a review on Amazon. It would be greatly appreciated!

Thank you and good luck!

Anthony Zagelow

If you seek further information about the author or wish to obtain consultation and design services, please visit: www.anthonyzagelow.com

Click Here to Download Your _FREE_ Copies of our Greywater Harvesting Guide & Sustainable Living Strategies Checklist